The Complete Guide t

TOTAL
TRANSFORMATION

Workbook

Table of Contents

What Is Holding You Back from Creating Lasting Change?

Even when faced with a life-threatening situation, people tend to resist change, despite knowing the repercussions. Why?

First, even bad habits are rewarding. Second, our brains are wired with an error alert system that sees new experiences as a threat, causing anxiety and fear in an attempt at stopping us from moving forward.

Because of our programming, there are several specific obstacles that can get in the way of deliberate change. Which of these do you feel hold you back?

- ☐ **Fear of Rejection/Judgment/Being Different:** This is ultimately the need for approval.
- ☐ **Fear of Uncertainty/Discomfort:** We are hard-wired to seek comfort and certainty and avoid failure.
- ☐ **Stuck in Habits/Patterns:** We are creatures of habit who value routine.
- ☐ **Overwhelm:** The tendency to suffer from disorganization, lack of clarity, and catastrophic thinking.
- ☐ **Confidence and Self-efficacy:** The lack in belief in their abilities or inability to trust themselves.
- ☐ **Fear of Disappointment/Failure:** Lack of faith that it will work out and fear of not meeting our own expectations, or others not meeting our expectations.
- ☐ **Fear of Unintended Consequences:** Change begets change. When one area of life is changed, it impacts other areas. Sometimes it requires other changes, and those changes may be scary or unpleasant. Sometimes changes impact other people and it can be hard and emotional straining to handle their reaction.
- ☐ **Lack of Clarity/Motivation:** The tendency for people not to know what they want or why they want it.
- **Other:**

The 6 Human Needs

At the core, our decisions and behaviors are driven by underlying needs and our beliefs about how these needs must be met. The 6 human needs are a powerful psychological framework, created by therapist Cloé Madanes and popularized by Anthony Robbins' strategic intervention strategies. These core needs are at the root of our motivations and why we prioritize certain decisions and actions, often without our awareness. Each person values one or more of these needs more than the others. Which need is your primary driver is a huge determining factor for how you live your life.

> The 6 human needs are:
>
> 1. Certainty/comfort
> 2. Uncertainty/variety
> 3. Significance
> 4. Love and connection
> 5. Growth
> 6. Contribution

The first four needs are called the needs of the personality. These four needs are things that we always find ways to meet them—they are vital. The last two are called the needs of the spirit and are needs not always met. In most cases, the first four needs must be met before a person is able to start to value and focus on meeting the last 2 needs. However, when we meet those higher-level needs is when we truly feel fulfilled. Explore which of these needs is your top priority. There may be 2 that stand out as more important to you than the others.

Need 1: Certainty/Comfort

At our core we want to feel that we are in control of our reality. This feeling gives us security. This allows us to feel comfortable in our life to feel that we can avoid pain and create pleasure. At the core this is just a survival mechanism that we have. Certainty makes us feel safe, emotionally, psychologically, and physically. Depending on how much we value certainty will depend how much risk we take in life. You probably have met people on both ends of the spectrum—those who want to control every single detail in their life and those that crave uncertainty. The extreme need for certainty, however, will hold you back because all growth and change requires uncertainty.

Need 2: Uncertainty/Variety

The second one is uncertainty. Yes, it's the opposite of the first one. Think about it—what would happen if you always knew everything that would happen to you? You would probably be bored to death. So, uncertainty brings excitement and spice to life. The level of uncertainty that you are willing and able to live with determines how much and how fast you will change. Keep in mind that being able to deal with uncertainty is also a skill that can be developed, as you become more confident that you can deal with change. Also, as you start associating uncertainty and change with something that create happiness and helps you achieve your dreams, your desire for certainty will increase.

Need 3: Significance

Think about it, we all want to feel like we are special. We want to feel like we are important, needed and unique. There are a variety of ways that we can get significance. For example, you can get it by feeling like you are the best at something, by making a lot of money, having the best house in your neighborhood, by buying the latest thing, getting a master's degree or a doctorate, by becoming a social influencer, by being the best dad, having a bunch of tattoos, you can even be that person that has more problems that anyone else, the most intimidating, or even the most spiritual person. As you can see that there are endless ways to feel significant. People will go to great lengths to feel significant in their life.

Need 4: Love & Connection

The next need is Love and Connection. Whether we realize it or not, love is that thing that we need more than anything. When we love 100% we feel alive and it is a powerful force. For love, many people are willing to do extortionary things for others, whether it's the love that a parent has for a child or the love of a romantic relationship. However, if we don't feel like we can get love, we settle for connection—even if these connections do not serve us. There are a lot of ways to get connection, whether it is through a friendship, a pet or even connecting to nature. Less-constructive ways of getting connection are through social media, sacrificing our authenticity to conform to a group, or people pleasing.

Need 5: Growth

The next one is the need for growth. Think about it if you're not growing in an area of your life, then that area is dying. This can be your relationship, your business, or an aspect of your personal life. If you are not growing than it does not matter what you are creating in your exterior world. That need for certainty can hold you back from growth, leading you to feel empty and not be able to feel true fulfillment. Growth can be scary because it can have uncertainty for some, but it brings fulfillment.

Need 6: Contribution

The last one is contribution and its one that many people reflect on in the later stages of life, as we look at our legacy. Contribution is like a higher level of the need for significance, the difference being that it's no longer about you. However, contribution is the essence of life. Life is not about me… it's about us. We are social creatures and we have a natural need to feel that we have a higher purpose and that our life has meaning. The way we find that is to contribution to others. In fact, the feeling that we are contributing to others can helps us overcome the biggest changes if we think it has a purpose. Life therefore is about creating meaning, and that comes from giving.

So, which need a person values most, and which ones they are starving to meet, will influence the choices that they make in life.

The power of identifying your own hierarchy of needs (which one/s are most important to you) is that you can then reflect to see if you're meeting your needs in constructive ways. (And, if not, consciously choose more constructive ways of meeting your needs.) In most cases, the lower level needs HAVE to be met in order for a person to turn their attention to the higher level needs.

Constructive ways of meeting these needs:

- **Certainty**: You can have certainty by having a daily routine or having a community around you that is supportive no matter what's happening in your life.
- **Variety**: You can have variety by adding diverse experiences to your life. You can also try new things and learn new skills.
- **Significance**: You can meet the need of significance by using your talents and skills. You can also master a skill and share your skills with others.
- **Love/Connection**: You can meet this need by establishing lifelong friendships spending more time with likeminded people, as well as improving your relationship skills.
- **Growth**: You can meet the need for growth by constantly learning. For example, reading new books, watching YouTube videos, or following others that help you grow. You can also surround yourself with people that motivate you and challenge you to become a better person.
- **Contribution**: You can meet the need of contribution by sharing your talents and passions with others. You can also engage in causes that are meaningful to you.

So, ask yourself:

- Which needs are the most important to you?

- How do you currently meet these needs?

- Which area of need are you currently struggling with the most?

- In what way do you feel like your need is not being met?

- What do you believe is necessary for your need to be met?

- How can you meet these needs in a way that will help you truly be fulfilled?

It's Breakthrough Time! Breaking the Change Cycle

Most people find deliberate change to be a difficult process. Many well-intentioned people have changes they want to make in their lives, but they get stuck repeating the same "change cycle" over and over again. Below you'll find this common cycle, and you'll most likely find it to sound oddly familiar because most people experience this process of inspiration and resistance when they face a decision to change.

Where are you stuck in the change cycle?

1. **Discontent**—You grow increasingly unhappy and discontent with an area of your life. You "hang in there," tolerate, ignore, repress, or otherwise deal with the circumstance because it is comfortable and familiar, and you fear change.
2. **Breaking Point**—Eventually your level of discontent builds high enough that you cannot take it anymore. You reach a "breaking point," either through exhaustion or due to a dramatic event occurring that triggers the break.
3. **Decision**—You decide you're ready to change and declare that you will no longer tolerate the undesirable situation. You take the first step toward change, giving you a short-lived sense of hope.
4. **Fear**—Usually, shortly (or immediately) after your feelings of empowerment, you encounter your fear. You become uncomfortable and anxious about the idea of changing. You doubt your decision. Both options look bleak. You feel helpless, empty.
5. **Amnesia**—The fear of change grows strong enough that it makes the original situation look much better than you originally thought. You perceive the original situation as less anxiety-producing than the change. You're used to it; it's comfortable; it's familiar. Plus, it has become part of your identity, so you resist letting it go. You temporarily forget why you wanted to change it so badly.
6. **Backtracking**—Most people choose to go back to or stick with the item they wished to change. You essentially talk yourself out of changing.

Which method do you want to use to break the cycle?

1. **Extreme Pain**: You have a breaking point that is severe enough to push through the change cycle. For many people, unfortunately, it takes an extreme circumstance to push them to evolve, such as major financial loss, job loss, loss of a loved one, the ending of a relationship, a severe accident, or a nervous breakdown. You see, your Higher Self knows what you truly want and will lead you to it. If you resist changing long enough, something will happen in your life that will put you in a position where you have NO CHOICE but to change.
2. **Self-Honesty**: You have the humbling experience of realizing that there's a part of you that doesn't really want to change. You are comfortable with your habits, with what you know. You have a lot of fear that holds you back. You have many self-limiting beliefs. You receive some sort of benefit from staying where you are. You are unhappy because you want to be unhappy. You are addicted to the situation. You believe your pain is you; it's your story. You can see your resistance to letting it go. Only after reaching this level of self-honesty can you truly choose to change.

Self-Honesty Reflection

Can you see how this change cycle has impacted your life? How?

```

```

Are you ready for it to stop? ☐ Yes ☐ No

Have you experienced change amnesia before? If so, when?

```

```

What will happen if you continue NOT to change?

```

```

Are you ready to swallow the pill of self-honesty, even if it is hard, because you are tired of being dissatisfied? ☐ Yes ☐ No

Are you ready to take responsibility for your life and create the life you dream of having?
☐ Yes ☐ No

Are you at the point where you will accept nothing less than what you truly want? ☐ Yes ☐ No

In order to be able to break the cycle, you also need to understand the underlying reasons you've been allowing yourself to keep avoiding change. If any of them apply to you, make a note of how you feel.

- You don't want to change.

```

```

- You don't know what you want. (Try imagining what you would want if time, money, and people did not limit you.)

```

```

- Your dream isn't big enough. (What would you do ANYTHING to attain?)

```

```

- You're letting your fear be bigger than you. (Are you really willing to settle?)

- You are attached to your problem. (What would you talk about without it? Who would you be?)

- You're benefiting from your problem. (What are you holding onto? How does it benefit you to NOT change?)

Your Hero's Journey

Your Hero's Journey Activity

Look at the 12 steps of the hero's journey and how it relates to your own life. There are no right or wrong answers here. Simply reflect on each step and check in with yourself to see what experiences from your own life you can relate to that stage of the journey. You may have experienced more than one journey in your lifetime. Every time there is a calling—a problem that pulls you to face a challenge or change—the hero (you) is being beckoned to a new adventure. You can go through this activity imagining it starting early in your life and addressing the first big challenge you faced, or you can address the most recent challenge—the one you might be experiencing right now. And in the end, your answers to the questions about your experiences within each stage may not fit together chronologically. The story might not unfold like a movie. In fact, it probably won't. But that's not the point. The point is that by looking at your life this way, you will be able to see that you, too, are on the path of a hero. You, too, will transform and fulfill your destiny. Trust the journey.

Step 1: Ordinary Life

Most of the time, the hero starts out living a normal, every-day life. Everything is familiar, comfortable. They feel uneasy, uncomfortable, dissatisfied. Then, something happens that wakes them up to the fact that something is wrong.

In your life, what were the first stirrings of dissatisfaction or unease? What happened to wake you up to the need for change?

Step 2: The Call

Depending on the hero, the problem could be external—such as a catastrophe happening in the world around them. For others, the problem is internal, such as becoming aware of a deep dissatisfaction with some aspect of life. After being exposed to this information, the hero feels called to do something about it. The hero is challenged to take action and step into the unknown.

In your life, what are you feeling called to do? Remember, this could be a calling that already happened or that is happening now. (This could be many things: advance your career, pursue a passion, improve your health, change a relationship, start a business, support a cause, etc.)

```


```

Step 3: Refusal of the Call

Often, at first the hero fails to answer the call. They are afraid of what it will take. They don't think they can do it. They think it will be to hard. They feel insecure, inadequate. Their familiar life of comfort calls them to resist this new adventure. They hesitate. But, they become increasingly aware that there are real consequences if they do not act. Something meaningful will be lost.

In your life, what fears or resistance did you experience after becoming aware of the problem that is/was calling you to action? What additional situations or information were you presented with that further helped you see what was at stake? What are/were you going to lose?

```


```

Step 4: The Guide

In most stories, the hero meets a guide, a mentor, or a helper that provides vital advice and points them in the right direction. The timing of the appearance of the guide varies, and so if the hero refuses the call, often a helper of some type appears to nudge them into answering the call. Sometimes the guide continues to return to the hero to help them move along their journey, however the guide never "saves" the hero or do anything for them. The hero does not need to be saved. But, at the same time, the hero never does it all alone.

In your life, who have been your guides? You can list all people who have influenced you, including mentors who do not know that you see them as a guide, such as authors of books you read. However, make sure to identify what guidance you have received that SPECIFICALLY relates to this story. Throughout the rest of the steps in the journey, make a note any time a guide (the same guide or new ones) provides additional advice or direction.

Step 5: The Threshold

This is the pivotal moment when the hero officially leaves the ordinary world and steps into the journey in a way that they cannot turn back. This is the decision point. This is when the hero begins their quest!

In your life, what decision point have you experienced? (Are you there now?) What IS the threshold—the pivotal moment? Imagine you stepped from your old life into your new life— what would be that actual step? (This could be an internal decision, a public commitment, a phone call, physically going someplace, making a purchase, enrolling in something, something symbolic, etc.). What exactly IS your quest? What would you call it? Give it a name.

Step 6: The Road of Trails

The entire purpose of a quest is for the hero to learn, grow, and, well, become the hero. In order for this to happen, there are inevitably obstacles to overcome, challenges to meet, and tests of strength of will. The hero will learn the rules of this new world. There will be moments of victory and moments of defeat. The hero will meet allies who help them face their foes. This is the action and adventure part of the story that keeps people engaged, wanting to know more. If the hero just went right from the decision to the victory, no one would watch. And it wouldn't make for a very fulfilling real-life story either. There is always more meaning in the underdog story, right?

In your life, what obstacles or challenges have you faced (or are you facing)? How has your strength of commitment and will been tested? What are the rules of this new world? How are they different from your old life? What victories have you had? In what ways have you failed? Who are your allies? Your enemies?

This is the turning point, when the hero finally goes all-in. They reach the point when they are 100% certain what must be done. They are ready to accept the risks and the possibility of failure. This second decision point happens when the hero approaches the innermost cave. This next threshold can be something literal, such as having to enter the cave which contains what the hero fears most or the ultimate challenge the hero must face. It can also be something symbolic, such as entering into the hero's darkest places, their inner conflict, their demons. The hero prepares to face the one, big thing that they have been putting off. Often the hero rests briefly to reflect on the journey and summons the courage to face the treacherous road that awaits. Tension escalates in anticipation of the ultimate test.

In your life, what is the innermost cave? What is the one, big challenge? What decision must you make? If you find yourself at this point now, this is the perfect time to be reflecting on your journey, which gives you the courage to see how far you've come and that your life has been preparing you for this moment. You are ready. How are you feeling? If you were the guide, what would you tell the hero at this moment?

Step 8: The Ordeal

This is the ultimate test. In movies, this part is called the climax—it's the peak of the action. The hero must face their greatest fear or face their most terrifying foe. One way or another, the hero must face death, whether literal or figurative. The hero uses the skills and experiences they picked up along their journey through the challenges and their innermost cave in order to face this final challenge. It's the hero's moment of truth. Everything is put on the line and the hero moves forward knowing nothing will ever be the same. It can't, this must be done. And looking back, it is obvious that this moment was inevitable.

In your life, what is the "death" you will face? (The fear, the situation, or the foe.) What skills and experiences have you picked up along your journey that will serve you now? What, exactly, must you do? Can you see that your entire life has been leading up to this moment?

Step 9: The Transformation and Reward

The hero defeated the enemy, survived, overcame. But more than anything, the hero transformed, like a butterfly emerging from its cocoon. Out of the ashes of death rises a phoenix of symbolic rebirth. The hero receives a reward in some from, whether it is recognition, power, wisdom, reconciliation, a treasure, but in the end, no matter the price, the true reward is always the glory of personal transformation itself. The real change is internal.

In your life, what will this transformation look like? How will you feel? What will be different? How will you be different? What reward will you enjoy? Why will it all have been worth it?

Step 10: The Road Back

The hero cannot relax and enjoy the thrill of victory for long. The hero feels another call—to return home—to share the spoils of the reward or bring what was learned to those they care about. The journey is not over. With reward in hand and transformation in heart, the hero charts the path back. But the road can be filled with additional risks and dangers. A villain may appear who seeks to steal the reward. Unresolved issues must be dealt with. The hero may face their shadow. These additional roadblocks challenge the hero to internalize what they've learned and prove to themselves that they have, in fact, changed for good. It is in this stage of the journey that the quest is won, or lost.

In your life, what does "returning home" represent? How are you going to use what you have learned or accomplished? Who will you help or what will you do with it? At this point, what unresolved issues do you anticipate having to face? What other obstacles do you anticipate will pop-up in response to your transformation? What shadows may be lurking?

Step 11: Rebirth

This is the moment the hero crosses the final threshold—the final test of the hero's true growth. The hero is tested for the final time—it is their moment to demonstrate their mastery and step into their power. This battle pushes the hero to defeat their limitations and release their old self, once and for all. They return home a hero.

In your life, after transforming, defeating your foes or reaching your goals, what final battle may you need to face? Is there another step in this journey that you need to take in order to fully be able to feel as though you are "home" and able to integrate everything you've learned in your life? What would it take to embrace your new self, 100%?

Step 12: Return with the Elixir

When the hero returns to his ordinary world, a changed person, they will have something to share with those back home. This could be a solution to a problem, a new perspective of life, a resource, or some sort of resolution with key players. Sometimes the hero faces doubters or is even punished for the journey. But, in the end, the hero always shares what they've learned or acquired with those who they did it all for. That is, after all, what makes them a hero.

In your life, what is the elixir you are bringing back with you from your journey? Who are you going to share it with? How are you going to pay forward what you learned? What difference are you going to make in the world? Will there be any haters or doubters? If so, how can you remind yourself that you didn't do it for them, you did it because it was your destiny to be the hero of your own life.

Regardless of where you find yourself along your personal adventure, the hero's journey shows you that you are always exactly where you are supposed to be. All you need to do is take the next step.

And as your journey continues to unfold, remember that it's not about avoiding problems, it's about what you learn while overcoming them. It's not about perfection, it's about progress. It's not about becoming famous or popular, it's about becoming YOU. And it's not just about you, also about how you use your life experience to make a greater impact.

Journey on.

What Do You Really Want?

Identifying What You REALLY Want

So, what do you want? If you're like most people, this is surprisingly difficult to answer. Most people are so inundated with messages from their parents, peers, and society of what they "should" want that their true desires are drowned out. Plus, even if they've held dreams and desires in the past, their life experiences have lead them to believe that what they want is not possible, and so they stop allowing themselves to want it. They tell themselves "I can't have that" and it hurts to want something they cannot have, and so they stop thinking about it. They give it up. They settle.

But, the good news is that dreams can never die—deep down you know what you want. It tugs at you from within, but you may be so used to ignoring it that you no longer notice.

Forgotten Dreams

What do you REALLY want? Answer this without allowing other people's opinions or beliefs limit you. Answer this without thinking about limitations—imagine for a moment that money is not an issue and that whatever that is currently blocking you is magically taken care of.

What are things you wanted, desired or dreamed about that at some point you decided you could NOT have and so stopped wanting them? This could have been in childhood or adulthood. You may not have allowed yourself to think about these desires in a long time. For each one, ask yourself if this is something that you STILL want. If not, cross it out and let it go. Circle any desires that you feel a strong emotional reaction to when you think about them.

17

Identifying What You Do NOT Want

For many people it's easier to identify what they do NOT want than what they DO want. When asked what they want, many people respond "not this!" So, to start, simply make a list of the things you know for sure you do NOT want in your life. These can be things that USED to be in your life that you never want to experience again. They can be things CURRENTLY in your life that you would like to stop. They can be things you are simply certain you never want in your FUTURE.

Once you know what you do NOT want, it will help you identify what you DO want. Ask yourself, "What is the opposite of what I don't want?" or "If I know I do NOT want _____, then it means that I do want _____."

I do NOT want:	I DO want:

Getting More Specific

You have determined some things you want and don't want. You have determined the roles, beliefs and ego states that have influenced your life story and the new perspectives you can now take of them. Now, it is time to delve into greater detail about what you WANT your life to be. You can always add to this activity later, as you learn more about your desires. Later you will rewrite the story itself, but here you are asking yourself what you want in your life and why.

AREA	WHAT DO I WANT?	WHY DO I WANT IT?
Home		
Partner/ Relationship		
Family		
Career		
Leisure		
Money		
Health		
Other		

"Yes, I want more of this!"

Once you begin asking yourself about what you want, you'll find yourself noticing more and more things that make you think, "yes, I want this!" It's okay if you're still not sure what you want. Allow your desire to grow over time. Throughout your day, simply notice whether you like or dislike certain things, people, situations or experiences.

Say, "Yes, I want more of this!" to the things you like.

Say, "No, thank you." to the things you do not like. Saying "thank you" acknowledges that you appreciate the ability to identify what you don't want because it helps you know more clearly what you DO want.

Digging Deeper into "Why"

Now we're going to ask you to dig deeper into the answers you provided in the "why" column. This is important because only if you have a **big enough reason** will you be committed to creating lasting change. And, the only way your reason to change your life will be big enough is if you understand your core reasons. Below is an example that will help illustrate the point.

A student in one of our classes once told us, "I can't wait to go home and start using these efficiency techniques to make my work more effective and productive" And so we asked, "Well, why do you want to be more productive?" The student said that it would help her to get a promotion at work. We asked her why she would want a promotion and she said "So I can get a raise." So we asked again, "Why do you want a raise" and she said "Because I need the money to buy a larger home". So we asked "Why?" and she says because I want my mother and sister to move in with me". "Why?" "Because it has been our dream to own a big house together and live together as a family."

To which we responded, "Good, NOW you have identified what you really want. It's a large house with your family living with you. You don't really want to be more efficient. What you want is the experience of having your family living with you."

Look at the reasons you wrote for "why" and ask yourself the following questions:

Why does this matter to you?

```
┌─────────────────────────────────────────────────────────────┐
│                                                             │
│                                                             │
│                                                             │
└─────────────────────────────────────────────────────────────┘
```

Why?

```
┌─────────────────────────────────────────────────────────────┐
│                                                             │
│                                                             │
└─────────────────────────────────────────────────────────────┘
```

How would it make you feel?

```
┌─────────────────────────────────────────────────────────────┐
│                                                             │
│                                                             │
└─────────────────────────────────────────────────────────────┘
```

What would happen if I didn't have, do, or be this?

Why does that matter?

Why?

Keep probing and asking yourself until you get to the core of the issue.

In some cases, you will find that your deeper motive is a specific desire, like in the example above. However, often the core motivation beneath your desire is actually an emotional state that you wish to experience. In fact, everything we want is because we believe it will make us *feel* the way we desire: good, or at least *better*.

Get Other People Out of Your Head

Lastly, consider if any of the things you "want" are truly only because you think you "should" want them. It's easy to unknowingly adopt other people's dreams. Get other people's voices and beliefs out of your head... then take a final look at your desires and confirm that this is TRULY what you want. Would anything change if you took other people's opinions and "shoulds" out of your desires?

The Wheel of Life: Identifying What Areas Need Your Attention

The Wheel is a simple but powerful tool designed to help you get a graphical representation of the present balance between different areas regarding your life and business which will most benefit you by improving.

The eight sections in the Wheel of Life represent different aspects of your life. Seeing the center of the wheel as 1 and the outer edges as 10, rank your level of satisfaction with each life area by filling in that piece of the pie to that level.

You can use the 8 categories in this sample or determine the 6 to 12 most important categories in your life and business to create your own wheel.

Use the following questions to help you determine how you would rate each life area on a scale of 1 to 10.

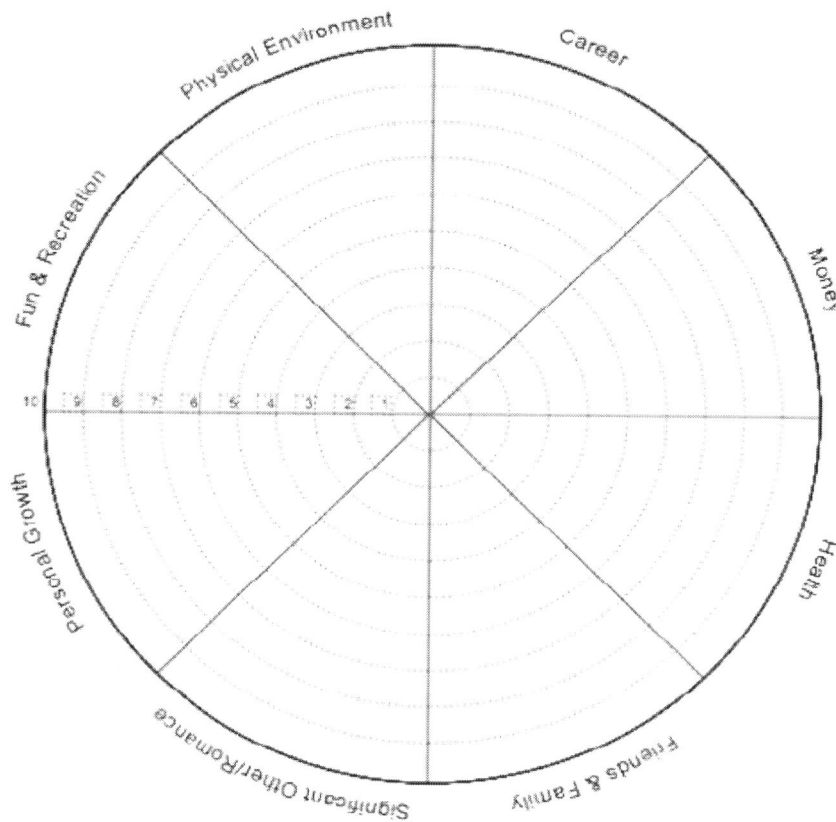

Career (Business)	Money
Is my business rewarding? Does it reflect my values? Do I feel balanced, in control, and happy with my time, responsibilities, etc?	Do I earn enough through my business? Am I happy with how I spend it? Am I on a path to financial freedom?
Health	**Significant other/ Romance**
Am I generally fit and well? Do I eat healthily? Do I exercise regularly?	Do I have/want a good relationship? Do we share values and intimacy? Am I nurturing the relationship and giving it the attention it needs?
Friends and Family	**Personal Growth**
Do I have/want a close circle of friends? Do I spend enough time with family and friends? Do I value the relationship we have with each other?	Am I continually learning new things? Do I enjoy new opportunities for growth? Are the things I do growing me as a person?
Fun and Recreation	**Physical Environment**
Do I have fun often? Do I know how to relax? Do I enjoy sports or have hobbies or take time for myself?	Do I like the area in which I live? Is my home comfortable, tidy and warm? Is my office conducive to productivity?

Interpreting Your Wheel

If this were a real wheel, how bumpy would the ride be? In theory, what you are aiming for with your completed wheel is to have all segments scored evenly (or close), above 7 and as near 10 as possible. Because not all areas are EQUAL in priority to you, consider marking each with a priority ranking of 1 (low) to 10 (high). Also, when determining how you rank each segment, rank each by asking "how balanced and satisfied am I with this one area" rather than comparing it to others. *Remember, balanced does NOT mean EQUAL.*

If you have any particularly low scores you will want to make those areas of your life a priority. However, it's not always cut and dry. It is necessary to investigate how they may interact with each other in order to identify the area to address first.

Questions to Determine Goals

Use the following questions to dig deeper and uncover your desired outcomes and what you can do to improve your balance.

- Have you ever been higher than the number you have recorded? ☐Yes ☐No
- What was actually happening when you were higher up the scale?

[ ]

- Have you ever been lower than the number you have recorded? ☐Yes ☐No

- What did you do to move up the scale?

```


```

- What have you learnt from previously being lower on the scale?

```


```

- What number on the scale do you want to be?

```


```

- What exactly do you want?

```


```

- What actions can you take to start moving up the scale?

```


```

- What will you be like when you have achieved this?

```


```

- What will be the impact of achieving this on other areas of your life?

```


```

- How will achieving this affect others close to you?

```


```

- What will achieving this bring you that you want?

```


```

- What will achieving this bring you that you don't want?

```


```

- What skills do you already have that will assist you in achieving this?

- What skills do you want to gain that will assist you in achieving this?

- Where can you learn these skills?

- What other options do you have?

- What would need to happen for you to move up one point on the scale by this time next week?

Who Do You Really Want to Be?

Identity Check-In: Who You Truly Are vs. Who You Are Being

If you imagine your life like a play, you would see that you play a character in this play. This character is a ROLE that you are playing. In fact, the character has multiple roles that it plays.

Make a list of the roles you play in life. There are generally 2 categories: career and relationships. You most likely play multiple roles in the "relationships" category, such as parent, spouse, child, etc. You may play more than one role under the "career" category too, such as "programmer" and "manager".

Career

- What is your career? (Fireman, teacher, sales, programmer, etc.)

- What role do you play in that career? (employee, manager, entrepreneur, support-role, problem-solver, etc)

- What are the traits, behaviors, and qualities of a person who is playing this role "correctly"?

- What are the traits, behaviors, and qualities of a person who is playing this role "incorrectly"?

```



```

- How does how YOU act out this role compare to what you believe you "should" be doing?

```



```

- Where did you learn how to play this role? Who taught or demonstrated this?

```



```

- Do you truly believe that the definition you have identified for this role is "correct"? If not, how would you change it?

```



```

- Does it feel right for you to be playing this role the way you are playing it now? Does it feel right to be playing this role AT ALL?

```



```

- How would you need to play the role differently in order for it to be in integrity with your true self?

```



```

Relationships

- What roles do you play in your relationships? (father, mother, child, brother, sister, grandparent, boyfriend, girlfriend, wife, husband, friend, neighbor, etc.) YOU WILL WANT TO COMPLETE THE QUESTIONS BELOW FOR EACH OF THE MOST IMPORTANT ROLES YOU IDENTIFY.
- What are the traits, behaviors, and qualities of a person who is playing this role "correctly"?

```



```

- What are the traits, behaviors, and qualities of a person who is playing this role "incorrectly"?

> _(blank box)_

- How does how YOU act out this role compare to what you believe you "should" be doing?

> _(blank box)_

- Where did you learn how to play this role? Who taught or demonstrated this?

> _(blank box)_

- Do you truly believe that the definition you have identified for this role is "correct"? If not, how would you change it?

> _(blank box)_

- Does it feel right for you to be playing this role the way you are playing it now? Does it feel right to be playing this role AT ALL?

> _(blank box)_

- How would you need to play the role differently in order for it to be in integrity with your true self?

> _(blank box)_

Final Questions

- Who, if anyone, would be affected by you letting go of (or change) the roles that don't serve you?

> _(blank box)_

- What benefit do you get from maintain these roles the way they are?

- What benefits would you get from removing or changing them?

- Who you would be if the roles you don't want to play anymore were to disappear?

Identity: Archetypes

The word "archetype" was coined by psychologist C. G. Jung and he believed they were narrative patterns that exist within the human psyche. An archetype is the core of your personality and is influenced both by your in-born nature and your life experiences. Below you will find a simplified description of each archetype. You may find that more than one feels like it represents a core part of your personality or identity, however there is usually one that makes you feel "yes, this is me!"

Also, your core archetypes can change over your lifetime. Take note if you feel a certain archetype represents who you WERE versus who you are NOW. Then, consider if you're hanging on to any of the beliefs from your old archetype, that no longer serve you now.

The Dreamer:

- Life is for: freedom and happiness
- Fear: being punished unfairly, being bad or wrong
- Strength: faith and optimism
- Weakness: naïve, defensive
- AKA: innocent, romantic, utopian, naïve

The Good Neighbor:

- Life is for: connecting to others, belonging
- Fear: being left out, different, standing out, rejected
- Strength: empathy, down to earth, peaceful
- Weakness: loses one's own self, superficial
- AKA; good old boy/girl, silent majority

The Hero:

- Life is for: proving one's worth, courage
- Fear: weakness, vulnerability
- Strength: competence, courage, boundaries
- Weakness: arrogance, always battling, attracts people who need saving
- AKA: warrior, dragon slayer

The Caregiver:

- Life is for: protect, care for, rescue others
- Fear: selfishness and not being needed
- Strength: compassion and generosity
- Weakness: martyrdom, self-sacrifice, being exploited
- AKA: altruist, helper, saint, nurturer

The Explorer:

- Life is for: freedom to discover yourself through exploring
- Fear: getting trapped, conformity, emptiness
- Strength: autonomy, independence, ambition, integrity
- Weakness: aimless, lack of commitment
- AKA: seeker, wanderer, individualist

The Rebel:

- Life is for: breaking rules, revolution or revenge
- Fear: powerlessness or complacency
- Strength: outrageousness, radical freedom, disrupting status quo
- Weakness: crime, conflict, instability
- AKA: revolutionary, wild, outlaw

The Lover:

- Life is for: intimacy, connection, relationship and being attractive
- Fear: being alone, unwanted, unloved
- Strength: passion, appreciation, connection
- Weakness: people pleasing, losing self in others, dependency, attention seeking
- AKA: friend, team-builder

The Creator:

- Life is for: creating things of enduring value, making visions reality
- Fear: mediocrity, settling, the status quo
- Strength: imagination, problem solving, action
- Weakness: perfectionism, impatience
- AKA: artist, inventor, innovator, dreamer

The Jester:

- Life is for: living in the moment
- Fear: being bored or boring others
- Strength: joy, levity, play
- Weakness: wasting time, irresponsibility
- AKA: the fool, practical joker, goof off

The Sage:

- Life is for: seeking the truth, growth
- Fear: ignorance, being duped or misled
- Strength: self-reflection, intellect, seeking knowledge
- Weakness: studying to excess with no action, over analyzing
- AKA: philosopher, advisor, thinker, teacher

The Visionary:

- Life is for: understanding the laws of the universe, making things happen
- Fear: unintended negative consequences
- Strength: following dreams, big picture, future vision, win-win solutions
- Weakness: becoming manipulative
- AKA: catalyst, inventor, charismatic leader, medicine man

The Ruler:

- Life is for: control and power, winning
- Fear: chaos, losing control, being controlled
- Strength: responsibility, leadership, organization, goal oriented
- Weakness: being authoritarian, unable to delegate
- AKA: leader, manager, aristocrat

Which of these archetypes do you feel represent you the most?

What aspects match your personality the strongest?

Become Who You Were Meant to Be (Your Life Purpose)

Every human being has untapped potential. They are born with certain talents and traits, and their life experience teaches them skills and inspires passions within them. e can choose to look for the deeper meaning in the experiences of our lives. We can choose to identify our talents and passions and make decisions to put them to work in our lives. We can choose to develop our potential and make our unique impact in the world.

This exercise looks at your talents and passions as clues to who you truly are, you're greater purpose.

First, ask the following questions about childhood:

- What came naturally to you? What were you good at?

- What did you LOVE to do the most?

- What did you want to be when you grew up?

Then, ask the following questions about your earlier adult life:

- What do you wish you had done differently with your career or your life?

- What did you feel yourself drawn to over and over again?

- What did you used to do that you really enjoyed that you aren't doing any more?

Lastly, ask the following questions about your current life:

- What comes easy for you that may be hard for others?

- What have you become an expert at?

- What would other people say are your greatest qualities? Talents?

- What would you like to change in the world?

Looking at the answers to all of these questions, what does it seem like your life has been preparing you for? What is your greater purpose?

Becoming Your Best Self—How Would I Need to Think and Behave?

After evaluating the different roles you play (whether they're in your career, family, or elsewhere), which roles do you feel are the MOST important for you to *change* in order to fully embrace your BEST self?

For each role you wish to change, ask yourself the following questions:

- What needs to be changed about how I THINK about what this role is and who I am in it?

- What needs to be changed about my BEHAVIOR?

- Next, after looking at your talents and passions, what did you determine your life has been preparing you for?

- In what ways are you not currently living up to this greater purpose and mission in your life?

- How are you not using your potential?

- What needs to be changed about how I THINK about yourself, your life, and the gifts you have to offer this world in order for you to move forward in the direction of your greater purpose?

  ┌───┐
  │   │
  │   │
  │   │
  │   │
  └───┘

- What BEHAVIORS do you need to stop, change, or start in order to live in integrity with your best self? For instance:
    - What things that you enjoy doing, are great at, and make you feel alive do you need to do more of?

  ┌───┐
  │   │
  │   │
  │   │
  │   │
  └───┘

    - What are you passionate about that you want to spend more of your time focused on? How can you make your passions a priority?

  ┌───┐
  │   │
  │   │
  │   │
  └───┘

    - What do you need to learn more about or practice in order to use your gifts and go for your dreams?

  ┌───┐
  │   │
  │   │
  │   │
  └───┘

Developing a Mindset of Success (Growth Mindset)

Mindset Assessment

There are no right or wrong answers. Choose the option that best fits you.

I believe I can always change my talent, no matter how much I have to start with.

- ○ 1 Strongly Disagree
- ○ 2 Disagree
- ○ 3 Disagree Somewhat
- ○ 4 Agree Somewhat
- ○ 5 Agree
- ○ 6 Strongly Agree

I like working on things that make me think hard.

- ○ 1 Strongly Disagree
- ○ 2 Disagree
- ○ 3 Disagree Somewhat
- ○ 4 Agree Somewhat
- ○ 5 Agree
- ○ 6 Strongly Agree

I don't mind making a lot of errors when I first start learning something new.

- ○ 1 Strongly Disagree
- ○ 2 Disagree
- ○ 3 Disagree Somewhat
- ○ 4 Agree Somewhat
- ○ 5 Agree
- ○ 6 Strongly Agree

When something is hard, it makes me want to try harder. It doesn't make me want to give up.

- ○ 1 Strongly Disagree
- ○ 2 Disagree
- ○ 3 Disagree Somewhat
- ○ 4 Agree Somewhat
- ○ 5 Agree
- ○ 6 Strongly Agree

I know I can learn new things, but I don't believe I can change my intelligence.

- ○ 6 Strongly Disagree
- ○ 5 Disagree
- ○ 4 Disagree Somewhat
- ○ 3 Agree Somewhat
- ○ 2 Agree
- ○ 1 Strongly Agree

I prefer doing things that I can do well at without putting a lot of effort into it.

- ○ 6 Strongly Disagree
- ○ 5 Disagree
- ○ 4 Disagree Somewhat
- ○ 3 Agree Somewhat
- ○ 2 Agree
- ○ 1 Strongly Agree

I prefer to work on things that I can do perfectly or get right most of the time.

○ 6 Strongly Disagree

○ 5 Disagree

○ 4 Disagree Somewhat

○ 3 Agree Somewhat

○ 2 Agree

○ 1 Strongly Agree

If I have to try hard or put in extra work, it makes me feel like I'm not good enough.

○ 6 Strongly Disagree

○ 5 Disagree

○ 4 Disagree Somewhat

○ 3 Agree Somewhat

○ 2 Agree

○ 1 Strongly Agree

Add up the numbers that correspond to each of your answers. **Your Score:** _____

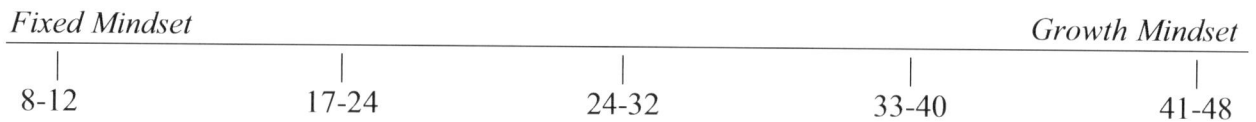

Fixed Mindset				*Growth Mindset*
8-12	17-24	24-32	33-40	41-48

What it Means

8-12: You strongly believe that your talents, intelligence, and abilities are fixed traits that can't be changed. You see putting in effort and trying hard as a sign that you just aren't good at what you're doing. If you are not likely to do well or succeed, you would rather not participate and instead choose to do things that come easy for you. You believe that talented or highly intelligent people are that way naturally and they do not have to put in effort to be that way.

17-24: You believe your talents, intelligence, and abilities probably don't change very much. You tend to choose situations in which you don't make many mistakes and you don't have to put in too much effort. You believe that learning and improving should be easy to do.

25-32: You're not sure if your talents, intelligence, or abilities can be changed, but you recognize you can learn and change in some ways. You care about your performance and being good at things, but you also value learning something new that you're not as good at, yet. You prefer not to have to try too hard.

33-40: You believe you can increase your intelligence and improve your talents and abilities. You care about learning and growing, and you're not afrait to put in effort to improve. You care about performing well, but you value learning, too. You would never avoid doing something in order to avoid looking or being bad at it.

41-48: You strongly believe that you can learn, grow, and improve in all areas, including your talents, intelligence, and abilities. You enjoy being challenged by things you're not good at, yet. You believe in the value of hard work, you don't fear making mistakes, looking bad, or even failing because you know these things lead you to learn and improve. You value performing very well and therefore you value the effort and learning it takes to succeed.

Remember: Your mindset can change and develop! You can shift your mindset more toward a growth mindset. Find out more at www.mindsetworks.com.

Developing a Growth Mindset Part 1: Awareness

Now that you know what a growth mindset is and why it is such an important belief system, you can begin to practice this way of thinking.

Awareness of Your Self-Talk and Fixed Mindset Triggers

Everyone has an internal voice, and part of this voice is an inner critic, inner hater, or inner doubter—it is the fixed mindset persona. You can hear this persona within the negative self-talk that happens in your thoughts and mind. It can sound like:

- I'm not good enough.
- I will probably fail.
- I can't do this.
- I don't want to risk it.
- I shouldn't have to try so hard.
- If I'm not naturally good at this, I should just quit.
- It's not my fault.
- This makes me uncomfortable, I'm not doing it.
- Why try if it won't change anything?

What does yours often sound like?

```



```

Give your fixed mindset persona a name. Naming it helps you remind yourself that this mindset—or habit of thinking—is not who you are!

I will call my fixed mindset persona: _____

Identify your triggers. What situations tend to trigger your fixed mindset persona?

- When you're thinking about taking on a big challenge or learning something new?
  ☐ always   ☐ sometimes   ☐ never
  What does your fixed mindset persona tell you when you're in this situation?

```



```

- When you're thinking about making a change?
  ☐ always   ☐ sometimes   ☐ never

39

What does your fixed mindset persona tell you when you're in this situation?

```
[                                                              ]
```

- When someone criticizes you?
    ☐ always   ☐ sometimes   ☐ never
  What does your fixed mindset persona tell you when you're in this situation?

```
[                                                              ]
```

- When you fail at something?
    ☐ always   ☐ sometimes   ☐ never
  What does your fixed mindset persona tell you when you're in this situation?

```
[                                                              ]
```

- When something goes wrong? Do you beat yourself up or blame someone else?
    ☐ always   ☐ sometimes   ☐ never
  What does your fixed mindset persona tell you when you're in this situation?

```
[                                                              ]
```

- When someone else makes a mistake? Do you judge them? Criticism them?
    ☐ always   ☐ sometimes   ☐ never
  What does your fixed mindset persona tell you when you're in this situation?

```
[                                                              ]
```

- When you're under pressure or on a deadline?
    ☐ always   ☐ sometimes   ☐ never
  What does your fixed mindset persona tell you when you're in this situation?

```
[                                                              ]
```

- When you procrastinate or are feeling lazy?
  ☐ always　　☐ sometimes　　☐ never

  What does your fixed mindset persona tell you when you're in this situation?

  ```




  ```

- When you have a conflict with someone?
  ☐ always　　☐ sometimes　　☐ never

  What does your fixed mindset persona tell you when you're in this situation?

  ```




  ```

- When your reputation is at risk or you worry what others will think?
  ☐ always　　☐ sometimes　　☐ never

  What does your fixed mindset persona tell you when you're in this situation?

  ```




  ```

Awareness of Your Reaction

Ask yourself, how am I rationalizing or judging the situation?

```




```

How am I beating myself up or blaming others?

```




```

What is the fixed mindset telling me?

```




```

Developing a Growth Mindset Part 2: Perspective

You may not always be able to change what happens around you, but you always have a choice of how you respond, react, and how you view the situation.

When you catch your fixed mindset persona with a limited thought, ask yourself, what else might be going on here?

```


```

What is a more realistic and optimistic way to look at this situation?

```


```

What are the good aspects of this situation?

```


```

How can I look at this differently?

```


```

Here are examples of rephrasing fixed mindset thinking as growth mindset thinking. Be on the lookout for any time you hear your fixed mindset persona taking over your internal dialogue, such as the reactions to the triggers you identified or the following common fixed mindset thoughts, you can change your perspective to a growth mindset,

- When you hear yourself thinking something like: "What if you're not good enough? You'll be a failure."
  Change it to: "Everyone starts out not being good and successful people all fail along the way."
- When you hear yourself thinking: "If it's this hard, you're probably just not good at it."
  Change it to: "If it's hard, it means I need to put in more effort and it will be a great achievement when I get good at it."
- When you hear yourself thinking: "If I don't try, I can't fail and I will keep my dignity."
  Change it to: "If I don't try, I have already failed and I have no dignity."
- When you hear yourself thinking: "It's not my fault."
  Change it to: "If I don't accept whatever part of this is my responsibility, I give away my power."

Go back through the fixed mindset triggers you identified and what your persona tends to tell you and rewrite a NEW thought from the growth mindset perspective.

My fixed mindset trigger thought:

My replacement growth mindset perspective:

My fixed mindset trigger thought:

My replacement growth mindset perspective:

My fixed mindset trigger thought:

My replacement growth mindset perspective:

My fixed mindset trigger thought:

My replacement growth mindset perspective:

Developing a Growth Mindset Part 3: Action

So, at this point you've noticed your fixed mindset persona thinking limited thoughts and you've changed your perspective. The next step is the most important, and in fact is what truly makes someone have a growth mindset. The most important factor for developing a growth mindset is action.

As yourself, what did you learn from the experience?

```



```

What could you do differently next time or going forward?

```



```

What would help you achieve this goal that you haven't tried?

```



```

What do you need to learn or what information do you need to gather?

```



```

What steps will you take?

```



```

DON'T STOP THERE! List out the steps that you will take, and for each one, identify exactly WHEN you will do it. If anything on your list cannot happen within 1 week, save it for later and re-assess at the end of the week. For everything else, include when you will do it and what you need in order to do it.

Lastly, **take 5 minutes to visualize yourself** taking each of these steps, as you imagine they will play out, including achieving the goal and outcome you are aiming for.

Practicing a Growth Mindset

Select your favorite affirmations from the list below or write your own and put them somewhere you will see them every day, such as next to your bed, on your mirror, on the cover of your day planner, attached to your computer screen, or programmed into the calendar of your phone to remind you to look at them every day, at least once.

- Everyone has a fixed mindset to some degree. Now that I know the difference and I know I can change, I am developing a growth mindset.
- Challenges, risks, and failures do not reflect that I am a failure, they are opportunities for me to grow and improve.
- I care more about the process and the journey and who I become along the way than I do about the outcome.
- I am glad that I am not perfect and that I never will be because it means I am not limited to where I am today.
- What other people think about me is none of my business. I no longer allow other people's opinions and judgments to hold me back from living a life of fulfillment and reaching my potential.
- I am always looking for the meaning and lessons contained in all situations that can help me fulfill the greater purpose in my life.
- I move past the discomfort of making mistakes quickly because I learn the lesson and allow it to help me improve so I can do better next time.
- I know that no one starts out great at something and so I am willing to try new things and practice skills I would like to have, putting in the time and effort I know it takes to master this area.
- I am the master of my thoughts, emotions, and actions and I do not give my power away by reacting to others criticism, judgment, or actions in a negative way.
- Having to exert effort in order to be good at something is a good thing because it shows me that I am capable of learning and improving. I love knowing I am not limited to my current strengths.
- I love knowing that even if someone else may be more naturally talented in an area than I am, a person with better work ethic will out perform a person with talent every time.
- I know that most truly successful people have failed their way to success.
- I have skills and knowledge today that I didn't have before because I learned and grew in those areas, so I know I can develop any ability I want.
- If my talents, abilities, and intelligence are not fixed, this means my potential is truly limitless!

Write your own:

The 3 Irrational Beliefs at the Core of Your Suffering

Why do we assign meaning to life event in the way that we do? The short, yet profound, answer is that all of our pain and suffering is caused by 3 core irrational beliefs.

Not all people hold the same variation of these beliefs, but we all believe them in one situation or another and these beliefs are always irrational. These beliefs are like internal rules that we have for how we, others, and the world "should" behave. The problem is that we normally are not aware that we have these beliefs. And if we do catch ourselves thinking these things, we don't normally question them.

By identifying which of these core irrational beliefs you tend to fall into the most, you can begin to become aware of the situations in which you apply these bogus rules. Below you will find a description of the 3 beliefs, as well as additional details that will help you identify if this belief is active within you.

BELIEF #1—APPROVAL: I must be approved of by others to be worthy.

- Need: acceptance, belonging
- Fear: judgment, rejection
- Demands: I expect myself to perform well and win approval from all significant others at all times, and if not I am a failure, unworthy, and deserve to suffer.

Symptoms:

- Places unrealistic expectations on oneself
- Over-concern with what other people think
- Achievement and popularity determine self-worth
- Self-critical, lack of self-acceptance

Emotional Consequences

- Depression, feeling not good enough, unable to express or embrace true self
- Anxiety, worry about what others think, being judged
- Low confidence, feeling bad about yourself, others disapproval means we are bad, can't be yourself

Behavioral Consequences

- Risk-avoidance, for fear of being judged for failing or being different
- Shyness, for fear of being embarrassed
- Procrastination, for fear of failure, judgment, risk
- Unassertiveness, for fear of rejection or criticism
- Workaholism, in order to gain approval

REPLACE WITH THIS RATIONAL BELIEF:

I have value as a human being simply by being my authentic self, and I desire love only from those who appreciate me and recognize the good in me.

BELIEF #2—JUDGMENT: Other people must do "the right thing" and meet my expectations in order to be worthy.

- Need: importance, superiority
- Fear: unfairness, disappointment
- Demands: expect all significant others to treat you kindly and fairly, as well as act appropriately, and if they don't they are unworthy, rotten people who deserve to be punished

Symptoms:

- Unrealistic expectations on others, including expecting them to be infallible, perfect
- Assuming you are the sole authority on what is right and wrong
- Assuming you have authority over others
- Believing everyone else is responsible for catering to your needs

Emotional Consequences

- Anger, rage or fury when others intentionally or unintentionally treat you poorly or unfairly or don't meet your expectations
- Impatience with others who make mistakes or aren't perfect
- Bitterness against others for not meeting your needs
- Resentment toward others for being imperfect and especially for treating you unfairly or not meeting your needs

Behavioral Consequences

- Aggression and violence as a way of punishing others for being inappropriate or not meeting expectations
- Bigotry and intolerance of anyone who does not meet your definition of right and wrong
- Bullying others to enforce your belief of the way others should behave or be
- Nagging others to elicit the right action you expect and require

REPLACE WITH THIS RATIONAL BELIEF:

All people, including myself, are imperfect, have value to offer, and have a unique perspective of the world.

BELIEF #3—COMFORT: Life must be easy, without discomfort or inconvenience.

- Need: certainty, comfort, justice
- Fear: adversity, uncertainty, discomfort
- Demands: expect all external conditions to be pleasant and favorable at all times and when they're not it is awful and unbearable.

Symptoms:

- Unrealistic expectations about life being perfect

- Belief that living a trouble-free life is a birthright
- Lack of belief in your ability cope with adversity
- Complete rejection of all life problems as unacceptable

Emotional Consequences

- Low frustration tolerance
- Self-pity and "poor me" attitude
- Depression, hopelessness
- Discomfort anxiety

Behavioral Consequences

- Procrastination
- Shirking
- Drug and alcohol abuse
- Overindulgence in "feel good" behaviors (e.g., overeating)

REPLACE WITH THIS RATIONAL BELIEF:

It is perfectly natural for life conditions to not be ideal or perfect and it's okay if situations do not exist the way I would prefer because I am capable of finding solutions to problems and making changes that bring me happiness and opportunity regardless of the situations that happen around me.

Which of these irrational beliefs do you feel you struggle with the most?

How do you experience it in your life?

Questioning Beliefs and Excuses

Questioning Beliefs:

The first step is to identify what you believe. Then, you'll look at where the belief came from, whether or not you know for sure it is true, and the impact it has on your life. In another video we'll look at how to change these beliefs. For each, ask yourself how you expect that they "are," "should be", or what they "mean".

Answer each quickly with your FIRST inclination.

BELIEF	Where did it come from?	Is it true? How do you know?	How does it negatively impact your life?	What would you like to change it to?
Failure means:				
Experiencing challenges means:				
Other people are:				
Money is:				
Work is:				
A career should be:				

The future is:				
Education is:				
Emotions are:				
Being a parent means:				
Being a child means:				
Being a man means:				
Being a woman means:				
Being single means:				
Being married means:				

Friendship means:				
Health means:				

Eliminating Excuses (Saying "No" to BUT!):

Below are several common excuses, including the truth that challenges them. Evaluate these beliefs for yourself and see what other excuses you tend to use so you can question them and empower your beliefs.

But, I'm not good at it. You're not good at it because you haven't practiced it! You're probably keeping this excuse around because you're afraid of failure. (See the Growth Mindset section for help with this one.)

But, People won't like/approve of me. You are not living life for anyone else. Sometimes you have to embrace the pack of haters if you want to live your dreams. You're probably keeping this excuse around because you're afraid of being judged. (see the 3 Irrational Beliefs video for help with this one.)

But, it's too hard. How would you know; have you done it? It's only too hard if you don't know how to do it. The good news is you can try it and learn. You're probably keeping this excuse around because it gives you an excuse not to try because it's not possible. (See the Growth Mindset section for help with this one.)

But, it's too risky. There are no risky changes, only risky people. If you prepare yourself, you can minimize risk. You're probably keeping this one around because if you don't take the risk you cannot fail.

But, it'll take too long. What is a "long time" anyway? If it is going to take 5 years, won't you be 5 years older whether you do it or not? You probably use this excuse to avoid having to make a decision or a commitment.

But, it costs too much. Now this not true in most cases. Chances are you are spending a ridiculous amount of money on something you don't need, like coffee, cigarettes, cloths—everyone has something they could give up to fund their dreams. Besides, everyone is capable of generating money with a side gig. Get creative! How COULD you afford to do this?

But, it's overwhelming. If you are feeling overwhelmed it's because you are trying to "bite of more than you can chew." You can't eat a big meal all at once. Make a plan for how you're going to get where you want to go but then focus on one thing at a time. (See the Creating Change: Practical Steps section for help with this.)

But, I don't have time. This is the most commonly used "but," and it is totally bogus. The truth is you are wasting time every day on unimportant things. Make it a priority and you will find the time.

But, it's not possible: Has anyone else accomplished it? Yes. Are they imbued with magical powers? No. We've heard so many times people who say "I've tried everything" but when asked what they tried the truth was that they tried the same 2 things over and over and gave up. The people who have accomplished what you want to do got there by doing something different than what you are doing. First of all, they tried. Second of all, they kept trying new things. And third, they learned what they needed and never gave up.

Which of the excuses above do you use the most? (There can be many.)

How does each of them tend to hold you back?

What other excuses do you tend to tell yourself?

How do these other excuses hold you back?

"If you don't go after what you want, you'll never have it. If you don't ask, the answer is always no. If you don't step forward, you're always in the same place."—Nora Roberts

Changing Beliefs (The Table Leg Method)

Imagine your belief is like a tabletop and the evidence that supports your belief is like the table legs. You look at the evidence and make a conclusion—a belief about it. Just like with a table, if you knock enough legs out from under it the belief will collapse. You do this by creating doubt about your evidence or looking at it in a different way. Then, after you collapse the old, unwanted belief that makes you doubt yourself or your dream, you can use the same method to build up a new one. That's right, it works in reverse! If you determine a belief that is more empowering that you'd prefer, you can find evidence that SUPPORTS your new belief. Add at least 3 legs and the table will stand.

STEP 1: Identify a limiting belief you would like to change:

Make a list of all of the things you can think of that provide evidence (table legs) that support your belief (at least 3 pieces of evidence).

STEP 2: Identify an alternative belief that is more empowering:

If you're having a hard time identifying a more empowering belief, ask yourself "what if I believed the opposite"? You want to choose a new belief that is believable. So, instead look for an IMPROVED belief. So, that could be "there is always opportunity in the market if you provide an exceptional product or service."

STEP 3: Unstick the emotional superglue:

Sometimes we become emotionally attached to our limiting beliefs. We experience benefits or emotional payoffs for keeping our limitations around, which makes them sticky. It is like supergluing the table legs to the floor.

So, ask yourself: what is the emotional payoff for holding onto this belief?

```



```

Be honest with yourself. Write down everything you can think of that may be an emotional or practical benefit.

```



```

Next, ask yourself: do these benefits outweigh the costs of keeping this limitation? ☐ Yes ☐ No

- If your answer is YES—that the emotional payoff is worth it—then you will most likely NOT be able to change this belief because you are too attached to it.
- If you answer is NO—the payoff is NOT worth continuing to be limited by this belief— well, then it's time to celebrate because you've just dissolved the superglue! You actually WANT to change, and that means it's time to start dismantling that table.

STEP 4: Create doubt by reframing your evidence:

Like we said, you believe what you believe because you look at the evidence and come to a conclusion. But what if the evidence was wrong, incomplete, or you just weren't seeing it clearly? That would make you question your conclusion, and that's exactly the point of this step. For **each piece of evidence** you identified for your limiting belief, ask yourself the following questions:

Could this be untrue?

```



```

Is there more to the story?

```



```

54

What is an alternative explanation?

The point is to question the evidence enough to create doubt. Some evidence will be harder to refute than others, but that's okay as long as you can knock out enough to leave less than 3 legs standing!

STEP 5: Find evidence to support your new belief:

Now we're gong to flip this around and build up the supporting evidence to solidify your new belief. Looking back at your desired belief, make a list of everything you can think of that supports this new belief. You only need a minimum of 3 but you want to create as many legs as possible so that this believe is way stronger than the old, limiting one.

With enough supporting legs, your new belief will stand. It might not be as strong as your old belief at first, but that is okay.

In many cases, the table legs that held up your old belief may have been really thick or really superglued because of the emotions tied to them. When thinking about evidence for your new belief, it may be harder to find emotionally-charged evidence, so you want to think of as many things as you can. The number of supporting legs will make up for the less powerful examples.

You've done it! You changed your limiting belief and replaced it with a new empowering belief! But that doesn't mean that the old limiting thoughts won't pop back up sometimes. You may need to remind yourself of this new belief multiple times, or even read it to yourself regularly, but through repetition you will be able to banish that limiting belief for good!

Developing Awareness of Emotions

If you want to re-gain your power to direct your own emotional state, you need to be able to:

- Notice you're experiencing an emotional state
- Identify what it is
- Know what to expect
- Know how to influence a new emotional state

Emotional States

Emotional States are actually 2 different things:

- The STATE is the physiological "feelings" that you experience
- The EMOTION is the psychological interpretation or "label" you put on the state

We experience complex states made up of chemical and hormone interactions that cause a variety of reactions in the body. Our emotions are the interpretations we make of these experiences—or the labels we give them.

So, based on what we talked about in Thoughts Create Emotions, we need to add a couple steps to the process.

Situation → Interpretation (thought) → State → Interpretation (label) → Emotion

What this means is the body responds to the thought first, then our minds interpret the reaction, label it, and an emotion is born.

The map is not the territory:

The labels we give emotions are like a box or a map. What's printed on the box may signal what's inside, but it is NOT what is inside. Just like a map may describe a territory, however it is NOT the territory. Maps are simplified, inadequate and ultimately flawed. It would be like eating a menu. In the same way, what we call "anger", the word, is not the experience. Saying you "love" someone hardly does the experience any justice. In fact, all words are simply signposts pointing toward meaning. The word "tree" is not a tree.

What IS an emotion if it's not map? Well, it's not a "thing" either. You see, labeling an experience as an emotion makes it seem like a NOUN. This is why many people believe emotions are things they HAVE or that happen TO them. The truth is that emotions are verbs (emoting is the verb)—they are a PROCESS. Fear is the process of fearing, which is a string of sensations that occur in a pattern. Fear takes many steps from observation or contemplation to processing and interpreting; then to physiological reaction and FEELING, and finally labeling it as fear.

If you obscure the process underneath a word label, you end up believing that emotions aren't under your conscious control. Once we recognize anger is a process, we recognize we have power over it.

Emotion Identification Chart:

Below are 6 common emotions and descriptions of the emotion, physiological state, and common resulting behaviors. This chart will help you get a general idea of the signs and symptoms of each emotion to make them easier to identify. Keep in mind everyone experiences each emotion somewhat differently and you may not experience all of the characteristics.

LABEL	EMOTION	STATE	BEHAVIOR
Happiness	Intense, positive feelings of well-being, pleasure, contentment, delight, joy, optimism, and gratitude. Affirmative, positive thoughts and mental clarity.	Head held high (posture), wide-eyed, smiling, laughing, relaxation of muscles, open body language.	Pleasant voice, friendly, swinging arms, dancing.
Boredom	Low-intensity, unpleasant feelings of apathy, restlessness, indifference, emptiness, and frustration. Defeatist thinking or wishing things were different.	Low energy, slumped posture, smirk or frown, low eyes, shallow breathing.	Resting head, fidgeting, staring.
Anxiety	Vague, unpleasant feelings of distress, uneasiness, stress, apprehension, and nervousness. Thoughts of uncertainty and worry, racing thoughts, difficulty concentrating and remembering.	Restlessness, sweating, clammy hands, hunched shoulders, swallowing, quickened breath, darting eyes, butterflies in the stomach, nausea.	Pacing, biting lip, fidgeting. Irritability, hypervigilance.
Anger	Intense, uncomfortable feelings of hostility and hurt. Feeling out of control. Thoughts of blame and resentment. Difficulty thinking clearly or rationally.	Muscle tension, headache, tight chest, increased heart rate, increased blood pressure, heavy breathing, clenched fist, furrowed brow, showing teeth, clenched jaw, sweating, trembling, flushed cheeks, large posture.	Loud voice, yelling, cursing, sarcasm, pacing. Sometimes leads to aggression, including hitting a wall, throwing an object, or lashing out at a person.
Sadness/ Depression	Feelings of intense pain and sorrow, guilt, unworthiness, disappointment, helplessness, gloominess, loss, grief, numbness, meaninglessness, loss of interest. Defeated thinking and difficulty concentrating and remembering.	Slumped posture and hunched shoulders, long face, slow movements, pouting, body aches, crying, shaking, crossed arms, fatigue, upset stomach, monotone voice.	Curling up into a ball, laying around, withdrawing, irritability.
Fear	Intense feeling of dread, impending doom, or panic due to a perceived danger or threat. Paranoid or worst-case thinking and hyper focused on the object of the fear.	Increased heart rate, increased blood pressure, alert eyes, high eyebrows, corners of cheeks pulled toward ears, clammy, sweating, quickened breath, goose bumps, butterflies in the stomach, shaky voice.	Freezing, fleeing, hiding.

Practicing Emotional Awareness and Identification

Next time you catch yourself experiencing an emotion that is distinct, ask yourself the following questions. Practice this line of questioning often, especially when experiencing unpleasant emotions.

- How do I feel?

- How do I know?

- What do I feel? Sensations?

- Where do I feel it? Locations?

- Where in my body did it begin? Move to?

- How do I recognize when OTHERS experience this emotion?

- Do I notice any of these signs in myself?

- What do I observe in my body language, vocal tone, thoughts, behaviors?

Affirmations and Incantations

4 Keys to Successful Affirmation Statements:
1. It must be believable and within your control
2. It must be present tense (happening now), personal (I), positive (no "not" or "don't")
3. You must FEEL IT
4. You must repeat it REGULARLY (3-5 times per day for 21-30 days)

What is a belief that you hold or a negative thought you say to yourself regularly that you would like to REPLACE with a more empowering, positive affirmative statement?

Write a NEW phrase to replace the old one, using the guidelines above. Repeat this affirmative statement at least 3 times a day (5 to 10 times each session). Consider posting it on your mirror, computer or nightstand where you can see it regularly. Do this with additional beliefs/thoughts.

Incantations

Incantations take affirmations a step further and make them PHYSICAL. An incantation is a phrase or language pattern that is said out loud and with an engaged physiology. Putting affirmations into motion engages more of your brain and makes it more real.

Incantations are also spoken OUT LOUD. This also sends additional signals to your brain that you are SERIOUS. If you must do your incantation when other people are around and you don't want to draw undo attention to yourself, you can do it silently—but whenever you can, say it out loud. Incantations can be a whole phrase like an affirmation, or they can be a short phrase such as "I am confident!"

What affirmation would you like to use as an incantation? Or, you can write a new one.

What movement could you make while reciting this incantation? (Examples: Raise your hands in the air like you're cheering, pull in your elbow as if you're saying "yes!", jump up and down or dance.)

Next, pick a certain time that you will practice your incantation EVERY DAY. Be specific so that it's easy to habituate it. For instance, you can do it right after you brush your teeth.

Reframing Your Thoughts

It truly is not what happened in your life that creates your story, it's how you interpreted (or framed) your experiences.

The Power of Interpretation (Perspective)

Your interpretation of events either empower you or disempower you. Even the worst experiences of life, that feel like a curse, can be re-framed to find the silver lining or blessing contained within them. It is the MEANING we attach to a situation that determines whether it moves us forward or holds us back. The meaning also impacts the way we react and feel about any circumstances.

Find the Silver Lining

For every seemingly negative circumstance in life, there either was (or could be) a positive outcome because of it. You can choose to interpret events in a way that is DISEMPOWERING (makes you feel resentful or guilty) or you can interpret them in a way that is EMPOWERING by asking yourself:

- "What else might be going on here?"

- "What did I learn from this experience?"

- "What can I do differently next time?"

- "What positive outcome eventually came as a result of this situation?"

- "What meaning does it have? What purpose does it give me?"

- "How can I use this for GOOD?"

Make a list of any experiences from your life story (past or present) that are "negative" and then identify the positive outcomes and/or the empowering perspective you can take from them.

"Negative" Life Experiences	Positive Outcomes/Perspectives

Preparing to Succeed

Identifying Possible Roadblocks

When working toward a goal or creating life change, it is inevitable that there will be roadblocks and setbacks along the way. There is a saying that goes, "when human makes plans, God laughs." Point being, it is not going to all unfold perfectly. There are two keys to overcoming barriers:

1. Being preemptive and preparing for possible problems
2. Develop an attitude of flexibility and creativity

First, look at what barriers are likely to come up. By identifying what might go wrong, you can prepare in advance, both with action and with mental preparation. Let's take a look at the most common roadblocks and how to overcome them. Which of these tend to happen to you?

Practical Things that Could Go Wrong: Considering your specific situation, what are some things that might go wrong? Think of as many things as you can.

Solution: Plan in advance whenever possible. Identify what you could do in the even that this happened, as well as anything you could do to prevent it. The trick to overcoming obstacles is to be prepared. Plan these action steps into your overall planning. (See the Creating Change Practical Steps section.)

My Experience:

Frustration/Impatience/Disappointment: Because of the inevitability that something is going to wrong, you are likely to experience negative emotions, such as frustration, impatience, or disappointment. These are, of course, completely normal emotional responses, but the key is to not allow them to stop you from moving forward.

Solution: Be flexible. Set realistic expectations. Accept that it is normal for things not to go exactly the way you want. Allow yourself to feel what you feel, but then take steps to find a better feeling perspective of the situation. Look for what can be learned. Explore other options.

My Experience:

Resources: Sometimes there may things you need, that you do not have, in order to accomplish what you're trying to do. These can be physical items, financial resources, access to space, or even an environment that supports your decisions.

Solution: The solution here is resourcefulness. If you don't have what you need, get creative with your ideas for how to get it. Plan in advance for what you are going to need. Ask for help. Brainstorm ways to generate extra money to fund what you need to do.

My Experience:

Other people/Support: The truth is that our changes impact other people, and often they don't like it. Other times, when we make changes and go for our dreams, it threatens other people's limiting beliefs about themselves, and they react with doubt or criticism. Because of this, there may be people who try to dissuade you from doing what you are doing. It may be challenging to find support. And it may be challenging to do what you know is right for you when you know it will make other people unhappy or they will judge you.

Solution: In the event there is a practical problem that your decisions will cause with other people, plan in advance for how you will handle it. In most cases, however, the issues with other people are actually internal—you simply don't like how you feel knowing other people don't like what you're doing. But, it is important to remember that you have to put the oxygen mask on yourself first. If you live your life according to other people's desires you end up burnt out and empty with nothing left to give. Also see the Social Influences and Saying No lectures. At the same time, if you are seeking support you may need to look outside of your immediate circle.

My Experience:

Time/Organization: One of the most common barriers is time. In the Questioning Beliefs and Excuses lecture we address that not having time is an excuse, not a true reason not to do something. While it may be true that you have a lot on your plate and many responsibilities, including work, school, or family, however there is always a way to find the time.

Solution: First, it is important to understand that time is mental concept more than a practical unit of measure. What keeps someone from having the time to do something is a lack of prioritizing it, not a lack of time. At a practical level, you can find the time by evaluating all of the activities you do throughout the day and considering what you could eliminate that is less important than this thing you wish to do. For most people, this includes things like watching television and social media. It may be different for you. Also, planning in the actions you need to take to accomplish your goal is vital. If you leave it up to chance, without a plan, it is not going to happen. See the Creating Change Practical Steps section.

My Experience:

```



```

Motivation/Confidence: The most detrimental internal obstacle for most people is lack of motivation and follow through, which in most cases stems from a lack of confidence that they are going to be successful.

Solution: The most important source of motivation is a strong, clear understanding of why you are doing something, which is addressed in the "Big Why" lecture. It is also vitally important to understand that you cannot create lasting change if you are depending on feeling motivated. Motivation is an emotion that comes and goes. Creating a concrete plan helps you stay on track even in those moments when you're not feeling motivated. Confidence comes from a belief in yourself that you are capable of learning and growing in whatever ways are necessary in order to achieve your goals, which is addressed in the Success Mindset section as well as the Developing Change Confidence lecture. By working on mindset and confidence, motivation is increased. Combine that with commitment to a concrete plan, and you have a recipe for success.

My Experience:

```



```

Willpower, Cues & Triggers

Don't leave it up to willpower. It is important to recognize that willpower is like a muscle, and that if we over rely on that muscle we may find it harder to resist triggers and therefore fail to create change. Dr. Roy Baumeister, a psychologist at Florida State University conducted studies on decision-making and willpower and concluded "self-control is like a muscle and that if you over exert the muscle it gets tired." You can try to will yourself to make changes, but temptations will drain you and make it harder for you to be able to make long-term changes.

Build Your Willpower Muscle

The willpower "muscle" is just like any other muscle—when you give it regular workouts, it grows stronger. The problem is that most people believe that willpower is that in-the-moment feat of self-control against an overwhelming craving or temptation. Exercising your willpower does not mean flexing your ability to torture yourself by sitting in front of warm, off-limits brownies. It does not mean telling yourself you are going to quit smoking and then hang around smokers at lunch. This does not work. True willpower comes when preparation meets commitment.

Commitment: Make a clear-minded decision regarding what you will or will not do, based on a clear understanding of why you want to do it and what will happen if you don't.

What have you decided you will or will not do?

```
[                                                                    ]
[                                                                    ]
[                                                                    ]
[                                                                    ]
```

Preparation: You cannot expect yourself to be able to resist temptation in the moment. Instead, identify what you need to do in order to be prepared! Answer the following questions:

- What do you need to do to be prepared?

```
[                                                                    ]
[                                                                    ]
[                                                                    ]
```

- Do you need any materials or equipment?

```
[                                                                    ]
[                                                                    ]
[                                                                    ]
```

- Do you need to change your schedule?

```
[                                                                    ]
[                                                                    ]
[                                                                    ]
```

- Do you need to remove anything from your home?

```
[                                                                    ]
[                                                                    ]
[                                                                    ]
```

- Are there scenarios or locations or people you need to avoid or be prepared to face with a pre-determined statement of why you will or won't be doing something?

For example, if you want to utilize your willpower to stop eating chips, throw out any that are in your home and commit to not buying any more. If you want to do 100 sit-ups every morning, don't leave it up to how you feel in the moment—instead, set an alarm reminder, put your matt in the right position the night before, and commit to do it when the alarm goes off, NO MATTER WHAT.

Regularly practicing different types of self-control: It has also been shown that if you practice self-control on smaller things it will build your willpower muscle. Identify simple things you can do to practice your self control. For example, waiting to check your social media, portion control on unhealthy snacks, keeping a food dairy, not responding to someone's comment that triggers you emotionally, sitting up straight, or any other thing that will help you to practice self-control

Visualize It

Mentally project yourself into the future—into a situation that is a trigger. Imagine the trigger happening but rather than imagining you responding like you normally would, instead imagine responding with the desired behavior. Practicing this mentally gives the brain a new framework. Once you can break a pattern in your mind, you'll be better able to break it when you are exposed to the trigger in real life.

The 3 R's of Habit Change

3 R's of Habit Loops

1. The Reminder: All our habits have triggers and these triggers initiates the behavior.
2. The Routine: This is the actual habit, action, or routine that you have.
3. The Reward: Is the benefit that you get from the actual behavior. Keep in mind that even negative consequences have benefits and serve as a reward.

Step 1: Set a Reminder for Your New Habit

Will you set a reminder using an alarm or notification? If not, what are some simple healthy daily habits that you already have that you do every day? How could you integrate your new habit into one of them?

```



```

Step 2: Make it a Routine

If your new habit is something you need to schedule in, where and how are you going to set aside time for it?

```



```

What else do you need to prepare in advance so that you have everything you need at the scheduled time to get up and go?

```



```

How can you protect this new routine?

```



```

Step3: Create a Reward

Does your habit have a built-in reward? If so, what?

```
```

What are some ideas of things you could do to reward yourself for meeting certain milestones? For example, every time you make it a week performing this new habit, you give yourself something special, whether it's something you do that you enjoy or a small gift to yourself.

```
```

The Psychology of Creating Change

Developing Change Confidence: The Change Resume

Life Area	Type	Situation/Change	Positive Outcome
	IDENTIFY AS: (1) Happened "to You" (2) "Bad" Change (3) "Self-Initiated"	Describe the situation or change.	Identify anything good that happened as a result, whether it eventually lead to something positive or if you learned something valuable.
EDUCATION: This could be changing schools, overcoming a fear, improving a grade, making an impact, changing friends, etc. **Change**: Transferred to a new school, 1980, 3rd grade **Positive Outcome**: Met my best friend			
FAMILY LIFE: This could be changes from any point in your childhood, such as: moving, breaking an arm, joining a club, learning an instrument, parents divorcing, or getting your first job, car, or boy/girlfriend. **Change**: Joined the t-ball team, 5th grade **Positive Outcome**: Learned how to get along with other kids			

WORK LIFE: This could be anything from getting a new job to getting fired to changing careers to going back to school. **Change**: Got fired from Bank of America, 1999 **Positive Outcome**: Ended up discovering a new career path I loved.			
ADULT LIFE: This could be going to college, breaking up or starting a relationship, getting married, moving, facing a fear, trying something new, learning something new, losing a loved one, divorce, a car accident. **Change**: Faced my fear of heights by climbing the Statue of Liberty **Positive Outcome**: Enjoyed the view, even though it was terrifying, and realized that I can handle my fear			

Quality vs. Safe Problems

Uncovering Quality Problems

So, the question is, how do you change this? The first step is identifying the quality problem and the safe problems you use as a way of avoiding the quality problem.

What are some problems you have in your life that you know you COULD do something about, but you don't ever seem to take the steps necessary to change it?

What quality problems—ones that may be harder to change but would dramatically improve your life—are you avoiding?

If you're not sure what the quality problems are, here is an activity to help you dig deeper into the life challenges you're experiencing to find the root.

It starts by asking yourself "why" repeatedly until you get to the core issue and there is no other WHY to answer. When you find yourself feeling frustrated, sad, angry, or otherwise facing an aspect of your life that you're unsatisfied with, ask yourself the following string of questions:

- What is the surface-level conflict or problem that you're experiencing?

- How do you feel?

- Why?

- Why does this bother you or affect you?

- Why do I feel that way about it?

And here are additional questions to ask to discover where the belief came from:

- Are there any benefits from feeling or reacting this way?

- What are they?

- Where or who did I learn it from?

- What benefits did they receive from it?

- Are they right? How do you know?

- What deeper level problem might be going on beneath the surface?

- What does keeping this problem around allow me to avoid?

Keep probing and asking yourself until you get to the core of the issue.

The Power of Pain and Pleasure

Everything we do in life is because we're either avoiding pain or moving toward pleasure.

If you're continuing an unwanted pattern, it's because you're associating more pain to stopping it than you are to continuing it. And if there's a change you keep putting off, it's because you associate more pain to making the change than keeping things the same. The truth is that you KNOW that making the change will pay off and be much more beneficial than staying stuck in old patterns.

Below is an activity that will help you stop unwanted patterns and make needed changes by associating massive pain with keeping around the OLD pattern and massive pleasure with making the desired change.

What is the PAIN you expect if you make this change? This can be pain from the experience of making the change and/or the pain you would experience if you DID reach your goal?

What is the PLEASURE you have experienced by NOT making this change? What benefit do you receive from keeping around this old pattern or this problem?

What is the PAIN that will happen if you DO NOT make this change? How will it impact your life, your career, your family?

What is the PLEASURE you will experience when do make this change and reach your goals and dreams? How will your life be better? How will you feel? What weight will be lifted? What other important outcomes will come from this?

73

The Power of Forgiveness

What is forgiveness?

Forgiveness is releasing the feeling that the other person owes us something and freeing ourselves from anger. You may believe that forgiveness is challenging, but when you understand who it is truly for—you—then it becomes easier. When you practice forgiveness, you will feel empowered. Forgiveness is freedom.

What forgiveness is NOT:

Many people do not forgive because they have a misperception about what forgiveness truly is. Therefore, let's go over some of the things forgiveness is not.

- Forgiveness is NOT: Reconciliation with the person.
- Forgiveness is NOT: Living in denial about a person's action(s).
- Forgiveness is NOT: Allowing the person to do the same behavior over and over again.
- Forgiveness is NOT: Having no consequence for a behavior.
- Forgiveness is NOT: Having the pain magically go away.

First, Forgive Yourself:

"True justice is paying once for each mistake. True injustice is paying more than once. Animals pay once, humans pay thousands of times. Every time we remember we judge ourselves and feel guilt over and over again." — Edgar Cayce

Many times, in our lives we make mistakes and we have to forgive ourselves for those mistakes. Most people have more resentment toward themselves than anyone else. There are two things that our minds unconsciously do when we feel guilty. One of them is to try to repay or make right our mistake, often excessively. If we feel that there is nothing we can do to make something right, the second option we choose (unconsciously) is to punish ourselves.

Take a moment to reflect on your actions (toward yourself or others) in the past that you may regret.

- Are there any mistakes you made that you continue to beat yourself up for? If so, what?

- How are you punishing yourself for it?

- Are you directly or indirectly punishing others for it?

[ ]

Your guilt is not going to undo what has happened. Even more importantly, holding onto this pain is causing further pain in your life. It is okay to let it go now. Release yourself from the burden of carrying it with you.

I forgive myself for:

[ ]

Apologize: If any of your self-grievances are towards others, consider expressing an apology through a letter, email, phone call, or in person. (Remember not to be attached to the results since this is about you, not them. Do not expect to be forgiven.)

[ ]

Next, Forgive Others

Write it down: Make a list of people you need to forgive and what you want to forgive them for. Include what you need to forgive yourself for.

[ ]

Reflect: Acknowledge the pain that the lack of forgiveness (on your part) has caused you and how it currently impacts your life. Is it more painful than the actual experience?

[ ]

Learn the lessons: What are some things that you can learn from the situations? Are there any positives that have or can come out of the experiences? What lessons could the other person(s) have learned?

[ ]

Let go: Release any expectations from anyone else. This includes expectations of forgiveness or apologies from others or changes in others' behaviors. Forgiving doesn't mean accepting unacceptable behavior, but if the person does not change it is your responsibility to free yourself from the pain of resentment and do what's right for you, even if it means cutting ties with the person. What expectations do you release?

Express Forgiveness: ONLY if you feel it would be beneficial to you, consider expressing forgiveness to another through a letter, email, phone call, or in person. (Remember not to be attached to the results since this is about you, not them. Do not expect an apology.)

Live and be free! Forgiveness is about personal power. A life well lived is your best revenge; therefore take your power back and focus on your desires. Don't do it because, "You'll show them," do it because you want to live your life with freedom and happiness. Forgiveness is often an opportunity to learn, grow, and heal. You may even find that the negative experiences were blessings in disguise if you can create a place for forgiveness and acceptance in your heart. Remember, forgiveness is 100 percent your responsibility. Only you can unlock the door to your prison and shift your life from limitation to freedom and joy.

Putting the Oxygen Mask on Yourself First

Most of us are taught that selfishness is bad. It's not true. Being willing to be selfish—and take care of yourself so you are at your best and, therefore, are able to bring your best self to the world and those you love—is the most selfless thing you can do.

If you look back at your life you'll see that there are times when you made decisions that truly honored YOU. Times when you did what you loved even if it was unpopular. Times you chose not to participate in something you knew wasn't right for you. Times you gave yourself a reward or took a much needed break. And because you made those decisions, you improved your psychological and emotional state. You became stronger. Your cup became full. You put the oxygen mask on yourself and, therefore, were able to support others. And you were better able to care for yourself and others.

- What decisions have you made in the past that honored you? How did they turn out?

- In what ways are you not honoring yourself or taking care of yourself?

- Are there situations in which you are self-sacrificing (or have) to the point of self-harm or

- What changes could you make that would help you put on your own oxygen mask on first, so that you're better able to assist others?

- What are some ways you could fill your own cup? What FEEDS you? What makes you feel fulfilled?

- What changes could you make that would stop beggars from being dependent on your filling of their cups?

- If you commit to filling your own cup, how will this change your life?

Overcoming Indecision, Autopilot and Being Stuck

Are you on autopilot?

What have you chosen to do because it was what you were "supposed" to do?

What did you really want to do that you didn't allow yourself to do?

What do you choose to do by default (like watching TV or being on social media)?

What else could you be choosing to do instead?

What do you actually WANT to do with your life?

Not knowing what you want:

In what areas of your life are you not sure what you want?

In what areas of your life do you get stuck at a decision point and just think, think, think?

Have you ever missed out on an opportunity because you didn't make a decision in time?

What decisions are you read to make now so that you do not miss the opportunity to choose?

Perfectionism:

What decisions have you struggled to make because you're waiting for it to be perfect?

What decisions have you held yourself back from because you're afraid of making the wrong decision?

What decisions are you ready to make now, accepting that the worst decision is not to move forward?

Being Indecisive:

Are you not sure which option to choose?

In what way could you try or test each option?

*If you can't actually try it out, run through the possibilities in your mind.**

Ask yourself, what are the possible outcomes?

How do I feel about each outcome?

For each outcome, what are the possible next steps?

After considering these options, what feels like the best choice for you?

Feeling Uncertain:

In what ways are you avoiding making a decision to move forward because you're not sure how it will turn out?

Is there a way you could try it out or find out more?

- If not, simply do it! You may never be able to predict the outcome.
- If you cannot get yourself to take action, see the Overcoming Inaction video.
- If fear is holding you back, see the Fear Setting video.

What decisions are you ready to make, even if you cannot know the outcome, knowing that you do not want to continue to put this off?

Are you facing any life-changing decisions or irrevocable choices?

What choice are you facing?

What is option #1?

What is option #2?

For each option, the result will lead to a different life. Imagine you are choosing to live LIFE #1 and allowing LIFE #2 to drift out to sea.

- What are the positive, meaningful **outcomes** I'll experience if I choose LIFE #1?

- What are the negative, meaningful **losses** I'll experience because I did NOT choose LIFE #2?

Now, switch your choice around in your mind, allowing LIFE #1 to drift to sea, and imagine what it would be like.

- What are the positive, meaningful **outcomes** I'll experience if I choose LIFE #2?

- What are the negative, meaningful **losses** I'll experience because I do NOT choose LIFE #1?

When you're 85 years old, which one would you regret NOT doing more? Why?

After doing this exercise, which option feels like it is best for you?

What can you do to honor, accept, and release the other option and be at peace with it?

Empowering Your Vision of the Hero's Journey

At this point, you are ready to fully move forward. Return to the Hero's Journey activity and reflect on any ways your story has changed. Do you see the story of what already happened to you any differently? Have you progressed further along the journey? What step to you feel you are at now?

This is the moment that the hero does the number one most important act that puts them in control of their destiny. The hero takes control of the pen… that writes the story… They take back their power from anyone that used to try to control their story. They take their power back from any obstacles that may exist, knowing there is always a path around them.

The hero looks at the trail ahead and sits down to write the rest of their story.

Going on Your Vision Quest

And that's exactly what you're going to do now—go on a vision quest. Looking forward at your next steps in the hero's journey and the dreams you have for your life, develop a vision of how your story will unfold.

Allow the steps in the journey to unfold in your mind, like a movie. Imagine what it will look like, feel like, and who will be there at different steps in your path.

Create as much detail in your mind as possible. You can do this with your eyes opened or closed. You can follow the steps in the hero's journey or allow the vision to unfold naturally.

When you get to the end of your quest, pause to really enjoy the moment. Imagine yourself celebrating your success, living authentically as yourself, and sharing your gifts with others.

What does it feel like to be the hero of your own life story?

Writing Down Your Vision

After you've imagined your quest unfolding, the next step is to write it down. You can use the hero's journey activity and fill in the steps, or you can write down a summary of what you saw. When writing down your vision, use the following 4 guidelines, called the 4 P's, to help your words speak directly to your unconscious mind in a way that makes your vision believable.

- Present Tense (as if it's happening now, not past or future—no "will" or "ed")
- Personal Perspective ("I" and "me" statements)
- Positive Language (avoid words like "not" or "don't")
- Passionate (put emotion behind it—remember the pain/pleasure)

You can make a visual representation of your vision or keep a copy of what you've create somewhere you can read it daily. As you continue moving forward along your journey, hold the image in your mind of WHO YOU TRULY ARE, standing in your power, determining your destiny with every step you make.

Journey on.

Creating Change—The Practical Steps

Identifying What It Will Take AND Getting on the Bridge

There are two ways to get on the bridge to your dreams:

1) **Take a small step:** What small step can you take today that officially starts you on the journey over the bridge to your dreams?

2) **Live AS IF you are already there:** What will it FEEL LIKE to be living in that state of authenticity, love, and meaning?

Below, do a recap of what you've discovered on your journey.

What are your top 2 human needs?

Where are you currently in the change cycle? Where do you tend to get stuck?

Where are you currently in your hero's journey?

What is the greater purpose you have discovered in your pain or challenges?

What are your top 3 TRUE desires?

What area(s) of your life are in need of the most transformation?

What are the most important roles that you need to change in order to be living in authenticity?

Which of the identity archetypes are you? How do you feel about this?

What did you identify as your greatest talents and gifts?

What are you the most passionate about?

What did you discover to be your life's mission—your greater purpose?

Who is your favorite role model? In what ways do you see yourself in this person?

After learning about your true ability to learn and grow in any area, how do you feel about your ability to change both the circumstances of your life and your behaviors and skills as well?

Which of the irrational core beliefs did you identify that you suffer from the most? How do you choose to think about this now?

What were the excuses that you identified that you use the most and that hold you back?

How do you think about each of them now, in a more empowering way?

[ ]

Did you determine any specific beliefs you wanted to change using the table-leg method? If so, what are the new beliefs?

[ ]

Have you changed any of your assumptions about reality?

[ ]

What are your favorite 1 to 3 affirmations or incantations that you created for yourself?

[ ]

What decisions have you made regarding how you are going to filter your exposure to influences in your environment and the people you surround yourself with?

[ ]

What are the top 1 to 3 roadblocks you identified and what solutions have you identified for how to prepare in advance for getting around them?

[ ]

What triggers or habits have you determined you would like to change? What are your plans for changing them?

[ ]

What strategies have you identified for practicing uncertainty to become more accustomed to the uncertainty of life change?

[ ]

What successes did you identify in the past (in your change resume) that inspire you to know that you CAN and WILL succeed through the life changes you are embarking on?

[ ]

Did you determine any deeper level issues that you were covering up with "safe" problems? If so, how do you feel now that you know what is really going on?

[ ]

What is the biggest benefit you identified of making these life changes?

[ ]

What is your biggest source of resistance?

[ ]

Why is the benefit SO MUCH MORE important to you than the resistance?

```



```

If you identified any decisions you are having difficulty making, which one do you feel you would regret NOT doing at the end of your life, and why?

```



```

Summarize the vision you created for your future:

```



```

What symbolic ceremony are you going to do in order to commit to your journey and/or celebrate your transformation?

```



```

Setting Long-Term Goals

Achieving any life goal requires knowing 3 things, which we refer to as "The 3 D's." In order to know these 3 things, you must ask 3 questions:

- Desire: What do you really want?
- Drive: Why do you want it?
- Do: What do you need to do? (which we'll get into in the coming videos)

Desire: What do you really want?

Step 1: Brainstorm: *Write down everything you can think of* (big or small) that you would like to change, achieve or do. For the sake of illustration, we'll be focusing on long term goals that are within a year. Your goal can be nearer or farther, but a year is a good timeframe to work with when discussing the activities in this program. If you have a goal that will take longer than 1 year, identify what part of it you CAN do in 1 year and write it down. Goals can be personal, work-related, or both.

Step 2: Simplify: Look at your list and group items that are similar or that can be combined into one larger goal.

Step 3: Prioritize: Look at your simplified goals and circle the ones you feel are your highest priority. Rate each circled goal on a scale of 1 to 3, 1 being the highest priority and 3 being the least.

Step 4: Identify 1 to 2 major goals for this year: Looking at your priorities, identify 1 to 2 goals that:

1. Will make the biggest impact on your life
2. Will take about a year to implement

My Top Goals:

1)_____

2)_____

SMART Goals

SMART GOALS are: **S**pecific, **M**easurable, **A**chievable, **R**ealistic and **T**ime Framed.

Specific: Is your goal(s) specific enough? Is it something that could be easily identified when you've reached it? If not, how could you make it more specific?

Measurable: Is your goal(s) measurable? Would you be able to tell you've reached it? Is there clear criteria? If not, how could you make it more measurable?

Achievable: Is your goal(s) achievable? Is it something that you've considered and understand that it is, in fact, possible and able to be accomplished? If not, how could you adjust your goal and/or timeframe expectations to make it achievable?

Realistic: Is your goal(s) realistic? If it's big and challenging, that's great, but is it something you are a) physically and mentally capable of doing, b) prepared for, and c) able to commit to? If not, is there another way to reach your goal, another similar goal, or something you can do to put this one within reach?

Time Framed: Does your goal(s) have a time frame? Have you set a date or duration? Do you have a sense of urgency for the next step? If not, is there anything else you need to do in order to be able to put your goal on a timeline and begin taking action?

One last step... OUTCOMES
Is your goal(s) written based on the OUTCOMES you want and not just the "task" you want accomplished? What ARE the outcomes you are looking for? Do you need to adjust the way you've worded your goals to be focused on outcomes?

Now, rewrite your goal(s) considering the SMART guidelines and based on outcomes:

1)_____

2)_____

Drive: Why do you want it?

Knowing Young "WHY": Look at the goals you've identified and ask yourself the following questions (for each goal):

Major goal:	Why is this desirable?	What is the desired outcome?	What will happen if this goal is not met?

Monthly Milestones

Charting the Course

Now that you've identified where you want to be in 1 year (your 1-2 major goals), you can chart a course to get there. The next step is to break down each major go into smaller sub-goals. This is called **"chunking"**. Think of your goals as the "big picture" and your sub goals or milestones as the bit-sized achievements that make your goal approachable and keep you motivated.

Identifying your monthly sub-goals helps you very clearly see the path to accomplishing your 1-2 major goals for the year.

The idea: Considering where you want to be in 12 months, start thinking about what would you need to accomplish in 9 months? And where would you need to be in 6 months to be on your way to the 9 month milestones? What about 3 months from now? Of course, you don't know exactly how and when everything will unfold—you are making your best guess.

The key to planning is to *make one*, while remembering that your plan will change.

Monthly Milestones: What are milestones or sub-goals you'll need to accomplish?

The first step is to break down your long-term goal into smaller milestones. This is called **"chunking"**. Think of your goals as the "big picture" and your sub goals or milestones as the bit-sized achievements that make your goal approachable and keep you motivated. You'll get into more detailed tasks and action steps later.

This process is like reverse engineering the outcome you want (your goal) to determine how you got there (your plan). Considering where you want to be in 12 months, start thinking about what would you need to accomplish in 9 months? And where would you need to be in 6 months to be on your way to the 9 month milestones? What about 3 months from now? Of course, you don't know exactly how and when everything will unfold—you are making your best guess. *The key to planning is to make one, while remembering that your plan will change.*

At the same time, looking at all of these goals can feel overwhelming. But, there is good news! You only have to focus on what is NEXT—not the whole process. Just like traveling across the country, you cannot take all the turns at once—they come one at a time.

- BRAINSTORM: For each of your major, yearly goals, make a list of all of the sub-goals you can think of. List everything you'll need to do, have or accomplish in order to reach this goal. (You may need to use additional space.)


```



```

Additional brainstorming space.

- GROUP: On the next page, you will group smaller sub-goals from above into broader categories or MAJOR MILESTONES. (Approximately 12.)
- ORDER: Put them in order—meaning, ask yourself what has to be completed FIRST, before other milestones can be worked on?

My Milestones:

1)

2)

3)

4)

5)

6)

7)

8)

9)

10)

11)

12)

60-Day Plan

Now it's time to create your short-term goals. Create a NEW list that focuses only on the first 2 months (60 days), or your first 2 milestones.

BRAINSTORM: What the tasks you will need to accomplish in the next 60 days (look at the next 2 milestones) in order to accomplish your sub-goals? Write down EVERYTHING you can think of.

- PRIORITIZE: Next you will arrange them in order of priority and what NEEDS to be done first before moving on to the other things. Circle the ones that need to be done first.

1-Month Plan

Take those priority items and put them in a list for month (below) 1. Put the rest in a list for month 2, and save it for later.

For each of these items, brainstorm ALL of the TASKS that will need to be accomplished in order to accomplish these sub-goals in 30 days. Write down everything you can think of. Detail is important here because these tasks need to be executable and not leave anything out.

Prioritize each item on a scale of 1 to 4 by writing the numbers next to each item. 1 represents the most important OR needs to be done before you can begin on other tasks and 4 being least important or time-sensitive. You now have the next 4 weeks' tasks (1 through 4).

Weekly and Daily Planning

WEEKLY PLANNING IS THE #1 MOST IMPORTANT ASPECT OF PLANNING.

A small percent of the population sets goals and creates plans that get them to this point. If you get this far, you're ahead of the game. However, most people who reach the point of having a plan for the month still don't accomplish their goals. Why? **WEEKLY PLANNING IS THE #1 MOST IMPORTANT ASPECT OF PLANNING.**

Why? Because THIS is where PLANNING meets ACTION. By their very nature, sub-goals in your 30, 60 or yearly plan CANNOT be action items NOW. But, you CAN take actions NOW that will keep you on your path to achieving these milestones.

Without a weekly plan, the week will unfold and no steps toward the goal will be made because existing responsibilities and other's priorities will fill the time.

Weekly Planning

First, determine WHERE you are going to put the action list, in a daily planner, on a white board where it can be seen, or in a planning or task app. Next, schedule a weekly strategy session. In order to establish the habit of a weekly strategy session, you absolutely MUST SCHEDULE IT IN! Even if you are working on your own, private, goals, choose a time that you will sit down for 20-30 minutes EVERY WEEK to plan the coming week's tasks.

Write Your "Ta-Da" List

Why do we call it a "ta-da" list? "To-do" sounds like an unpleasant list of tasks that you have to do, while "ta-da" is more inspirational. Every time we finish a task, we cross it off and say "ta-da!" Celebrating even the little victories gives us a sense of accomplishment and builds momentum. We enjoy it so much, in fact, that if we find that we've completed a task that we didn't already have on our list, we ADD IT to the list just so we can cross it off!

Take the Priority 1 items from your Monthly Plan and write them down as **Actionable Tasks.** If needed, break tasks even further into action steps.

- IDENTIFY TASKS: Take the #1 priorities you identified in your 30-day plan. Break down these tasks further if needed in order to identify everything you would need to do to accomplish these sub-goals this week
- PRIORITIZE: Identify which tasks are a priority (mark 1 through 3) and plan to do level 1 FIRST.
- PLAN: Schedule any tasks that are time-framed and assign other tasks to specific days of the week, when required. Keep the rest of your week's list someplace easily accessible to refer to throughout the week when identifying daily goals. (See video and worksheet for Daily Goals.)

- o If items need to be completed on a specific day, note this.
- o If items are priorities that absolutely must be completed this week, star or highlight them and focus on these FIRST.
- o As you accomplish things, cross them off. Keep them there to show you what you've done!
- o Remember that sometimes life happens and not everything on your list for the week will happen. That's okay, simply move it forward to the next week!

Create Your Daily Plan:

Every day, look at what you have on your schedule as well as your weekly Ta-Da list. Write in your sub-goals/tasks for the day, and then IGNORE EVERYTHING ELSE.

Today's Tasks (in order of priority)	NOTES

Symbolism & Ceremony

When experiencing life transformation, there are often milestones or significant moments that should be acknowledged. Acknowledging these important moments is a powerful way to not only reinforce the changes, but positively reinforce everything it took to get to that point. Some type of symbolic activity or ceremony is a great way to tell the unconscious mind that this transformation is official, real. At the same time, a ceremony can be used in advance of accomplishing the desired outcome, as a commitment to the process or a release of the past.

A symbolic ceremony can be conducted in person or in the imagination. Here are two examples:

- **Burning Ceremony:** Print or write either the accomplished goal or the old belief, behavior, or past activity that is being acknowledged and released. Read it, thank it for its role in serving to help you become the person you are today. Then burn it safely in a firepit, a can, or a patch of dirt. While it burns, celebrate that it is being released.
- **Visualization:** Close your eyes, take 3 deep breaths, and bring into your mind the story or images that represent what is being acknowledged and released, almost as if you're watching a movie. Then imagine turning off the movie, putting the film screen or DVD it is on into a small sail boat, and sending it off to sea. As you watch it gently drift away, acknowledge that you are releasing it and letting it go.

There are many other ways to create some form of symbolic ceremony to signify important milestones, life changes, accomplishments, or the release of something that is not serving you. You can write a letter to yourself, burn an item that represents the situation, tie a note to a rock and sink it, release balloons, release a floating lantern, gather a group of people and make public declaration, giving yourself a symbolic gift, and the list goes on.

What symbolic ceremony will you create for yourself?

For other workbooks and the online courses that accompany them,
visit www.transformationacademy.com.

Printed in Great Britain
by Amazon